The Art
of the Process

Establishing good habits
for successful outcomes

Beth Costello

For me, graphic design has been my career, and so much more. For more than 30 years, I have lived and breathed design every day of my life. I consult and collaborate with a diverse group of business clients on their creative projects. I teach graphic design to aspiring designers and students, and I inspire artists to expand their creativity through innovative art classes.

Through my experience, I have developed a process that I use as I take on each new creative project, which guides my project strategy and helps me work through challenges. As a graphic design instructor, I have recognized that a similar project organization tool can benefit designers on all levels—from beginners to tenured. Welcome to The Art of the Process, a ten-chapter workbook designed to guide any graphic designer through the specific stages essential to a creative project's success. This workbook will simplify the process, allowing you to reveal your true creative capabilities.

I dedicate this book to all aspiring graphic design students and professional graphic designers who allow their creativity to inspire and shape the world we live in.

Acknowledgments

To all the people who helped make this book a reality. Russ, Zachery, Dean, Emily, Amanda and a very special thanks to Cole, my constant creative support. Izolda Maksym and Lorri Elton whose professional advice on content leaves no stone unturned. Joan Accolla, whose creative insight and honesty is greatly appreciated.

Own Your Creativity

What You Need To Know

This book is intended to guide you through the graphic design process by giving you organized prompts necessary to help build your project and establish guidelines for designing.

How To Use This Book

There are ten-project chapters, in each project section...

1. Fill in or circle criteria needed
2. Answer creative brief questions
3. Set due dates and log hours worked
4. Brainstorm ideas
5. Begin preliminary design work
6. Sketch thumbnails
7. List or draw fonts, graphics and images
8. Create color palettes
9. Create a final sketch
10. Have fun with creative prompts and test your knowledge with art puzzles
11. Graphic Design Basics gives you information on what every designer needs to know.

Suggested Supplies
that work well on this paper

1. Pens
2. Pencils of all kinds
3. Colored Pencils
4. Micro pens
5. Light watercolor

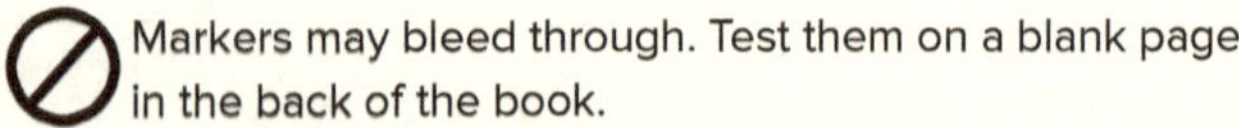

Markers may bleed through. Test them on a blank page in the back of the book.

Project
1

I find that students who take the time to work through the design process are more successful at time management and producing quality work.

Font: Goudy Old Style
Open Type

Project:

Client:

Client Contact: #

Printer Contact: #

Final Due Date:

What are you producing?

Print

☐ Logo   ☐ Brochure   ☐ Business Card   ☐ PSA

☐ Infographic   ☐ Flyer   ☐ Multi-page Booklet

☐ Postcard   ☐ Print Ad   ☐ Package Design

☐ Outdoor Advertising   ☐ Poster   ☐ Vehicle Wrap

☐ Other____

Web

☐ Social Media Ad   ☐ On-line Book   ☐ Website

☐ Animated Gif   ☐ Web Banner   ☐ Video

☐ PowerPoint   ☐ Image Corrections

☐ Other ____

Programs that will be used to build the project.

☐ Illustrator   ☐ Photoshop   ☐ InDesign   ☐ Quark Express

☐ PowerPoint   ☐ Premiere   ☐ Final Cut Pro   ☐ Corel

☐ Other_________________   Program Version _______________

Platform: Mac   PC

What is the purpose? (the objective)

What is the message? (main selling point)

Where will this product be used?

How will this product be used?

When will this product be used?

What is the tone of the piece? (use adjectives)

Who is your competition?

Who Is Your Target Audience?

Demographics - Gathering Data
Who do you want to buy your product or service?

Age

Gender

Occupation

Ethnicity

Income

Interests/Hobbies

Values

Religious Beliefs

Location - Suburbia, Rural, Metropolitan

Pacific

Rocky Mountain

Southwest

Mid-West

Southeast

Northeast

Schedule
(due dates)

Client Brief ___________________________________

Press Date ________________________________

Concept Web ______________________________

Thumbnails ______________________________

Sketches ________________________________

Project Presentation _______________________

First Revisions ____________________________

2nd Revisions _____________________________

Final Revisions ____________________________

Client Approval ___________________________

File Submissions ___________________________

Delivery Date______________________________

Log Your Hours

Date	Time	Total hours worked
/ /	_______________	_______________
/ /	_______________	_______________
/ /	_______________	_______________
/ /	_______________	_______________
/ /	_______________	_______________
/ /	_______________	_______________
/ /	_______________	_______________
/ /	_______________	_______________
/ /	_______________	_______________
/ /	_______________	_______________
/ /	_______________	_______________
/ /	_______________	_______________

Project Dimensions and Specs.

in   pica   px   mm   pt

Number of Pages ____

Size H ____________ x W _____________x D _______________

Size H ____________ x W _____________x D _______________

Columns ______________   Margins ___________________________

Bleed _________________   Gutter ___________________________

Color Mode   ☐CMYK   ☐RGB   ☐ Spot Colors

☐ Other_________________________________

File Formats

Print   ☐ ai ☐ psd ☐ indd ☐ eps ☐ tiff ☐ pdf
☐ svg ☐ jpeg ☐ other_________________________

Web   ☐ psd ☐ eps ☐ tiff ☐ gif ☐ png ☐ jpeg
☐ Other_________________________________

DPI ____

Other Specifications/Finishing

☐ spreads ☐ template ☐ die cut ☐ die ☐ mock up

☐ binding ☐ fold ☐ score ☐ perforation ☐ gloss

☐ matte   ☐ printer's marks: crop/registration/bleed

☐ other_______________________________x D_______________

Attention Grabbing Components Needed
(fill in content after you brainstorm)

Headline:

Subtitle:

Body Copy:

Slogan/Tagline:

Company Name:

Product Name:

Other:

Brainstorm - Concept Web
(word association)

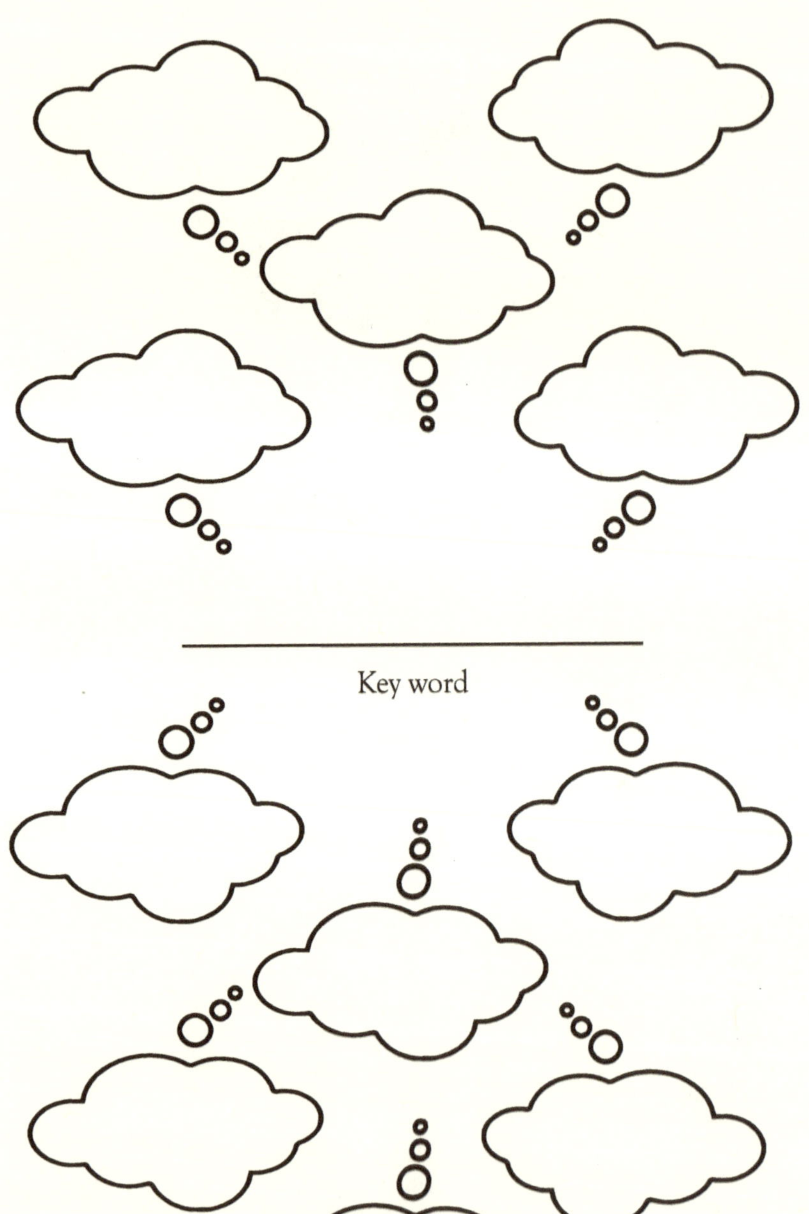

Organize Your Thoughts
(from the concept web)

Stumped?

Like the rings of a tree closely draw a circle around the dot. Repeat, expanding the size of each circle until you fill the entire page.

Thumbnails
(a thumbnail is a small sketch that captures an idea)

(a thumbnail is a small sketch that captures an idea)

Thumbnails
(freely draw the shape needed)

Don't make excuses!

Notes

Colors
(create the mood)

Palette #1

Palette #2

Texture/Pattern

Spot Colors

Typeface/Font Ideas
(Serif, Sanserif, *Script*)

Headline

1)

2)

3)

Subtitle

1)

2)

3)

Body Copy

1)

2)

3

What is the difference between a typeface and a font?

Graphics
(make a list, or sketch)

Graphics
(make a list, or sketch)

Photographs/Illustrations
(make a list or paste ideas from magazines)

Sketch From Thumbnail
(use the grid to align elements)

Final Design Choices

Color Palette

Headline Typeface & Alignment: ____________________________________

Subtitle Typeface & Alignment: ____________________________________

Body Copy Typeface & Alignment: ____________________________________

Graphics

1)   5)

2)   6)

3)   7)

4)   8)

Photography/Illustrations

1)   5)

2)   6)

3)   7)

4)   8)

Now you are ready to design on the computer.

Notes

1. *Are you sure you have exhausted all possiblilities?*

2. *Get yourself a flash drive to back up your work!*

3.

4.

5.

6.

7.

8.

PROJECT
[2]

This book is portable and easy to carry. Keep it with you always. Inspiration can strike at any time.

Font: Permanent Marker
True Type

PROJECT:

CLIENT:

DUE DATE

WHAT ARE YOU PRODUCING?

PRINT

- [ ] LOGO
- [ ] BROCHURE
- [ ] BUSINESS CARD
- [ ] PSA
- [ ] INFOGRAPHIC
- [ ] FLYER
- [ ] MULTI-PAGE BOOKLET
- [ ] POSTCARD
- [ ] PRINT AD
- [ ] PACKAGE DESIGN
- [ ] OUTDOOR ADVERTISING
- [ ] POSTER
- [ ] VEHICLE WRAP
- [ ] OTHER ____

WEB

- [ ] SOCIAL MEDIA AD
- [ ] ON-LINE BOOK
- [ ] WEBSITE
- [ ] ANIMATED GIF
- [ ] WEB BANNER
- [ ] VIDEO
- [ ] POWERPOINT
- [ ] IMAGE CORRECTIONS
- [ ] OTHER ____

PROGRAMS THAT WILL BE USED TO BUILD THE PROJECT.

- [ ] ILLUSTRATOR
- [ ] PHOTOSHOP
- [ ] INDESIGN
- [ ] QUARK
- [ ] POWERPOINT
- [ ] PREMIERE
- [ ] FINAL CUT PRO
- [ ] COREL
- [ ] OTHER ____________ PROGRAM VERSION _____

PLATFORM: MAC   PC

WHAT IS THE PURPOSE OF THIS PROJECT? (THE OBJECTIVE)

WHAT IS THE MESSAGE? (MAIN SELLING POINT)

WHERE WILL THIS PRODUCT BE USED?

HOW WILL THIS PRODUCT BE USED?

WHEN WILL THIS PRODUCT BE USED?

WHAT IS THE TONE OF THE PIECE? (USE ADJECTIVES)

WHO IS YOUR COMPETITION?

Who is your Target Audience?

Demographics – Gathering Data

Who do you want to buy your product or service?

Age

Gender

Ethnicity

Occupation

Income

Interests Hobbies

Values

Religious Beliefs

Location – Suburbia, Rural, Metropolitan

Schedule (Due Dates)

Client Brief _______________________________

Press Date _______________________________

Concept Web _______________________________

Thumbnails _______________________________

Sketches _______________________________

Project Presentation _______________________________

First Revisions _______________________________

2nd Revisions _______________________________

Final Revisions _______________________________

Client Approval _______________________________

File Submissions _______________________________

Delivery Date _______________________________

Log Your hours

Date	Time	Total hours
/ /	__________	__________
/ /	__________	__________
/ /	__________	__________
/ /	__________	__________
/ /	__________	__________
/ /	__________	__________
/ /	__________	__________
/ /	__________	__________
/ /	__________	__________
/ /	__________	__________
/ /	__________	__________
/ /	__________	__________

Project Dimensions and Specs.

IN   PICA   PX   MM   PT

Number of Pages _______________________________________

Size H ___________ x W ___________ x D ___________

Size H ___________ x W ___________ x D ___________

Columns _______________ Margins _______________

Bleed _______________ Gutter _______________

Color Mode: CMYK   RGB   Spot Colors

                  Other _______________________________

File Formats

Print   AI   PSD   INDD   EPS   TIFF   PDF

             SVG   JPEG   Other _______________________

Web   PSD   EPS   TIFF   GIF   PNG   JPEG

             Other _______________________

DPI ____

Other specifications/Finishing

        Spreads   Die Cut   Die   Mock Up   Binding

        Fold   Score   Gloss   Perforation

        Matte   Template   Printer's Marks

        Other _______________________________________

Attention Grabbing Components Needed
(fill in content after you brainstorm)

2

Headline:

Subtitle:

Body Copy:

Slogan/Tagline:

Company Name:

Product Name:

Other:

____

Main Idea

ORGANIZE
(FINAL THOUGHTS FROM THE CONCEPT WEB)

Stretch

Take a break and go for a stroll. It's good to step away from your project and refresh your creativity. When you come back, make a list of ten things you saw.

THUMBNAILS

Breaking out of a daily routine can help spark creativity. Take a different route home.

More Thumbnails

Colors
(create the mood)

Palette #1

Palette #2

Texture/Pattern

Spot Colors

Typeface/Font Ideas
(Serif, **Sanserif**, *Script*)

Headline Fonts

1)

2)

3)

Subtitle/ Supporting Fonts

1)

2)

3)

Body Copy Fonts

1)

2)

3)

Graphics
(make a list, or sketch ideas)

Graphics
(make a list, or sketch ideas)

Photographs/Illustrations

(make a list or paste ideas from magazines)

Sketch from Thumbnail

Final Design Choices

Color Palette

<table><tr><td> </td><td> </td><td> </td><td> </td><td> </td></tr></table>

ALIGNMENT

Headline Font: ______________________________

Subtitle Font: ______________________________

Body Copy Font: ______________________________

Graphics

1)   5)

2)   6)

3)   7)

4)   8)

Photography/Illustrations

1)   5)

2)   6)

3)   7)

4)   8)

PROJECT
3

Font: Copperplate
True Type

PROJECT:

CLIENT:

CONTACT NAME & NUMBER

DUE DATE

WHAT ARE YOU PRODUCING?

PRINT

LOGO   BROCHURE   BUSINESS CARD   INFOGRAPHIC   FLYER

MULTI-PAGE BOOKLET   POSTCARD   PRINT AD   PSA

PACKAGE DESIGN   POSTER   VEHICLE WRAP   STATIONARY

OUTDOOR ADVERTISING

OTHER____

WEB

SOCIAL MEDIA AD   ON-LINE BOOK   WEBSITE   ANIMATED gif

WEB BANNER   VIDEO   POWERPOINT   IMAGE CORRECTIONS

OTHER ____

PROGRAMS THAT WILL BE USED TO BUILD THE PROJECT.

ILLUSTRATOR   PHOTOSHOP   INDESIGN   QUARK

POWERPOINT   PREMIERE   FINAL CUT PRO   COREL

OTHER____________________   PROGRAM VERSION __________

PLATFORM: MAC   PC

WHAT IS THE PURPOSE OF THIS PROJECT? (THE OBJECTIVE)

WHAT IS THE MESSAGE? (WHAT DO YOU WANT TO SAY)

WHERE WILL THIS PRODUCT BE USED?

How will this product be used?

When will this product be used?

What is the tone of the piece? (use adjectives)

Who is your competition?

WHO IS YOUR TARGET AUDIENCE?
DEMOGRAPHICS - GATHERING DATA
WHO YOU WANT TO BUY YOUR PRODUCT OR SERVICE?

AGE_______________________ GENDER_______________________________

ETHNICITY____

RELIGIOUS BELIEFS____

OCCUPATION_____________________INCOME______________________

VALUES____

LOCATION____

SCHEDULE

	S	M	T	W	TH	F	S

CLIENT BRIEF _______________________________________

	S	M	T	W	TH	F	S

PRESS DATE _______________________________________

	S	M	T	W	TH	F	S

THUMBNAILS_______________________________________

	S	M	T	W	TH	F	S

SKETCHES _______________________________________

	S	M	T	W	TH	F	S

PROJECT PRESENTATION _______________________________________

	S	M	T	W	TH	F	S

FIRST REVISIONS _______________________________________

	S	M	T	W	TH	F	S

SECOND REVISIONS _______________________________________

	S	M	T	W	TH	F	S

FINAL REVISIONS _______________________________________

	S	M	T	W	TH	F	S

FINAL FILES _______________________________________

	S	M	T	W	TH	F	S

DELIVERY DATE _______________________________________

Log Your Hours

Date	Time	Total Hours Worked
/ /		
/ /		
/ /		
/ /		
/ /		
/ /		
/ /		
/ /		
/ /		
/ /		
/ /		
/ /		

3

PROJECT DIMENSIONS AND SPECS.

IN   PICA   PX   MM   PT

NUMBER OF PAGES ____

SIZE H ______________ x W ______________ x D______________

SIZE H ______________ x W ______________ x D______________

COLUMNS _____________________ MARGINS _____________________

BLEED ____________________________ GUTTER _____________________

COLOR MODE   CMYK   RGB   SPOT COLORS

OTHER ___________________________________

FILE FORMATS

PRINT   AI   PSD   INDD   EPS   TIFF

PDF   SVG   JPEG   OTHER_______________

WEB   PSD   EPS   TIFF   GIF   PNG

JPEG   OTHER_______________________

DPI ____

OTHER SPECIFICATIONS/ FINISHING

SPREADS   DIE CUT   DIE   MOCK UP   BINDING

FOLD   SCORE   GLOSS   PERFORATION

MATTE   TEMPLATE   PRINTER'S MARKS

OTHER _______________________

Inspiration

(paste images from magazines, mail or any printed material)

3

Need inspiration, look to the past to design for the future.

ATTENTION GRABBING COMPONENTS NEEDED
(FILL IN CONTENT AFTER YOU BRAINSTORM)

HEADLINE:

SUBTITLE:

BODY COPY:

SLOGAN/TAGLINE:

COMPANY NAME:

PRODUCT NAME:

OTHER:

Need a Break?

How many art terms can you find?

abstract	body copy	minimalism	Graphic Design
Romanticism	thumbnails	San serif	vector
Picas	target audience	raster	typography
jpeg	pdf	Dada	serif
font	web design	Art Nouveau	Bauhaus

3

```
q y p r i n t n y m o l p r c t g b f t
a r t n o u v e a u k m p d w q a n j y
s a c i p m o p b s z i r e y t o k h p
q c j i e f j n a m l n p r c z g b f o
b o d y c o p y u z k i p d w q a n j g
y m r v c m o p h w z m a e v e c t o r
q p j a e f j c a m o a p n c z g b f a
e u a l b m a v u z k l p d b q a n j p
y t r v c r o d s w z i r e y m o k h h
q e j i e f a n y m o s p r c z u b f y
e r a e d n g c i z k m p d w q f h j b
y c v p f m o p t w z m r e y i o k t b
q r j w e b d e s i g n p r r z g b f t
e o a l o m g v i z k o p e w q a n j b
y p r v c m o p b w z g s e g e p j h b
q m j i n g i s e d c i h p a r g b f q
t a r g e t a u d i e n c e w q a n j b
y r r v r o m a n t i c i s m t o k h d
p k y j i e f j n y m o l p r c z g b a
e s a l o m g v i z k f i r e s n a s d
y i r a s t e r b w z t n o f t o k h a
```

Brainstorm - Concept Web
(build your own)

Listen to your intuition. Write down the first word that pops into your head.

Organize Your Thoughts
(from the concept web)

3

Organize Your Thoughts
(from the concept web)

Thumbnails

Test your skill. How many thumbnails can you sketch on this page in 15 minutes?

More Thumbnails
(stretch your imagination)

Colors
(create the mood)

Palette #1

Palette #2

Texture/Pattern

Spot Colors

3

HEADLINE

SUBTITLE/ SUPPORTING

BODY COPY

To many fonts can distract. Consider using "styles" for contrast. (project dependent)

GRAPHICS & IMAGES
(MAKE A LIST, OR SKETCH IDEAS)

FINAL DESIGN CHOICES

COLOR PALETTE

HEADLINE FONT & ALIGNMENT:

SUBTITLE FONT & ALIGNMENT:

BODY COPY FONT & ALIGNMENT:

GRAPHICS

1)   5)

2)   6)

3)   7)

4)   8)

PHOTOGRAPHY/ILLUSTRATIONS

1)   5)

2)   6)

3)   7)

4)   8)

Project
4

Font: Calisto MT
Open Type

Project:

Client Contact & Number:

Contact Name:

Printer Contact & Number:

Due Date:

What are you producing?

PRINT

Logo   Brochure   Business Card   Infographic   Flyer

Multi-page Booklet   Postcard   Print Ad   Package Design

Outdoor Advertising   Poster   Vehicle Wrap   PSA

Other____

WEB

Social Media Ad   On-line Book   Website   Animated Gif

Web Banner   Video   Powerpoint   Image Correction/s

Other ____

Programs that will be used to build the project.

Illustrator   Photoshop   InDesign   Quark Express   Corel

PowerPoint   Premiere   Final Cut Pro   Other_____________

Program Version _______________________

Platform >   **Mac**   **PC**

What is the purpose of this project? (the objective)

4

What is the message? (what do you want to say)

Where will this product be used?

How will this product or service be used?

When will this product or service be used?

What is the tone of the piece? (use adjectives)

Who is your competition?

Schedule
(keep on task)

Client Brief _______________________________________

Press Date _________________________________

Concept Web _______________________________

Thumbnails ________________________________

Sketches _________________________________

Project Presentation _______________________

First Round Revisions ____________________

2nd Round Revisions ______________________

Final Revisions __________________________

Client Approval __________________________

File Submissions _________________________

Delivery Date_____________________________

Month ___________________________________

Sun	Mon	Tues	Wed	Thur	Fri	Sat

Time Sheet

Date	Time	Daily hours worked
______	______	______
______	______	______
______	______	______
______	______	______
______	______	______
______	______	______
______	______	______
______	______	______
______	______	______
______	______	______

Total amount of hours worked ______

Fill in your hourly rate x $ ______ .

Total Amount Due = ______

Target Audience
Demographics - Gathering Data
Who you want to buy your product or service?

Age

Gender

Ethnicity

Religious Beliefs

Occupation

Income

Interests & Hobbies

Values

Location

Project Dimensions and Specs.

in   pica   px   mm   pt

Number of Pages ____

Size   H ______________ x W ______________ x D______________

Size   H ______________ x W ______________ x D______________

Columns ________________   Margins ________________

Bleed ________________   Gutter ________________

Color Mode   CMYK   RGB   Spot Colors

Other ________________

File Formats

Print   ai   psd   indd   eps   tiff

           pdf   svg   jpeg   other________________

Web   psd   eps   tiff   gif   png

          jpeg   other________________

DPI ____

Other specifications/ Finishing

spreads   die cut   die   mock up   binding

fold   score   gloss   perforation   matte

template   printer's marks

other ________________

Inspiration
(paste images from magazines, mail or any printed material)

4

Inspiration can come from anywhere. A crack in the side walk, the laugh of a child, the movement of the ocean.

Blocked! Take a break

Match the artist to their Movement
How many can you match in a minute?

Paul Cezanne	Art Nouveau
Frida Kahlo	Pointillism
Henri Matisse	Post Impressionism
Frank Stella	American Modernist
Andy Warhol	Abstract Expressionism
Mary Cassatt	Fauvism
Alphonse Mucha	Impressionism
Jackson Pollack	Pop Art
Georges Seurat	Minimalism
Georgia O'Keeffe	Surrealism

Attention Grabbing Components Needed
(fill in content after you brainstorm)

Headline:

Subtitle:

Body Copy:

Slogan/Tagline:

Company Name:

Product Name:

Other:

List 5 Key Words
that reflect your company.

List 5 key words
that reflect how you want people to feel
when using your product or service.

Organize Your Ideas
(final thoughts from the concept web)

4

Thumbnails

A thumbnail is a small sketch that allows you to put your thoughts down on paper quickly. A computer can not do that!

More Thumbnails
(keep going, add color)

Colors
(create the mood)

Palette #1

Palette #2

Texture/Pattern

Spot Colors

Pantone Matching System (PMS) - Spot color, a color that is pre-mixed before being used in the printing process. Check out PMS 263

Typefaces/Fonts

Headline

Subtitle/ Supporting

Body Copy

Graphics & Images
(make a list, or sketch ideas)

Final Sketch

(the dots form a grid that will help you align the elements)

4

Final Design Choices

Color Palette #1

Headline Typeface/Font & Alignment:

Subtitle Typeface/Font & Alignment:

Body Copy Typeface/Font & Alignment:

Graphics

1)   5)

2)   6)

3)   7)

4)   8)

Photographs/Illustrations

1)   5)

2)   6)

3)   7)

4)   8)

Project
5

Creating thumbnails shows your thought process. It doesn't matter how many of them are silly or suck. It matters that you've exhausted all options before choosing the best one.

Font: Helvetica Light
True Type

<table>
<tr><td>

Project

Client

Contact Name   #

Printer Contact   #

Due Date   Budget

</td></tr>
</table>

What are you producing?

Print

Logo   Brochure   Business Card   Infographic   Flyer

Multi-page Booklet   Postcard   Print Ad   Package Design

Outdoor Advertising   Poster   Vehicle Wrap   PSA

Other____

Web

Social Media Ad   On-line Book   Website   Animated Gif

Web Banner   Video   Powerpoint   Image Correction/s

Other ____

Programs that will be used to build the project.

Illustrator   Photoshop   InDesign   Quark Express

PowerPoint   Premiere   Final Cut Pro   Corel

Other__________________ Program Version _____________

Platform >   **Mac**   **PC**

What is the purpose of this project? (the objective)

What is the message? (what do you want to say)

5

Where will this product be used?

How will this product or service be used?

When will this product or service be used?

What is the tone of the piece? (use adjectives)

Who is your competition?

Who Is Your Target Audience?
Demographics - Gathering Data
Who you want to buy your product or service?

Age
- Children
- Teenagers
- Young Adults
- Thirty Somethings
- Mid Life
- Seniors

Gender
- Female
- Male
- Gay
- Lesbian
- Bi-sexual
- Trans-gender
- Cross Dresser
- Drag Queen

Occupation:

Ethnicity:

Religious Beliefs:

Interests Hobbies
- Technology
- Sports
- Food
- Nature
- Travel
- Clothing
- Health & Fitness
- Other

Values
- Family
- Education
- Creativity
- Compassion
- Travel
- Clothing
- Health
- Happiness
- Generosity
- Other

Income
- $ 0 - 20,000
- $20,000 - 35,000
- $36,000 - 50,000
- 51,000 - 75,000
- 76,000 - 100,000
- Other

Location
- Metropolitan
- Suburbia
- Small Town Rural
- Motor Home
- Boat
- Homeless

5

Due Dates & Time Clock

Client Brief _____________________ Press Date _____________________

Concept Web _______________ Thumbnails ___________________

Sketches __________________ Project Presentation ___________

First Edits _________________ 2nd Edits ___________________

Final Edits________________ Final Project Submission _________

Final Files Sent ____________ Delivery Date________________

Date	Time	Daily hours worked
_________	_________	_________
_________	_________	_________
_________	_________	_________
_________	_________	_________
_________	_________	_________
_________	_________	_________
_________	_________	_________
_________	_________	_________
_________	_________	_________
_________	_________	_________

Total amount of hours worked _________

Project Dimensions and Specs.

in   pica   px   mm   pt

Number of Pages ____________________

Size   H ______________ x W ____________ x D___________

Size   H ______________ x W ____________ x D__________

Columns ________________   Margins ___________________

Bleed ____________________   Gutter ____________________

Color Mode   CMYK   RGB   Spot Colors

Other ______________________________

File Formats

Print   ai   psd   indd   eps   tiff

pdf   svg   jpeg   other______________________

Web   psd   eps   tiff   gif   png   jpeg

Other______________________________________

DPI ____

Other Specifications/ Finishing

spreads   die cut   die   mock-up   binding

fold   score   gloss   perforation   matte

template   printer's marks

other ___________________________

Inspiration

(paste images from magazines, mail, or any printed material)

Don't overlook the obvious. There is potential in all that we see.

Attention Grabbing Components Needed
(fill in content after you brainstorm)

Headline:

Subtitle:

Body Copy:

Slogan/Tagline:

Company Name:

Product Name:

Other:

Brainstorm - Concept Web

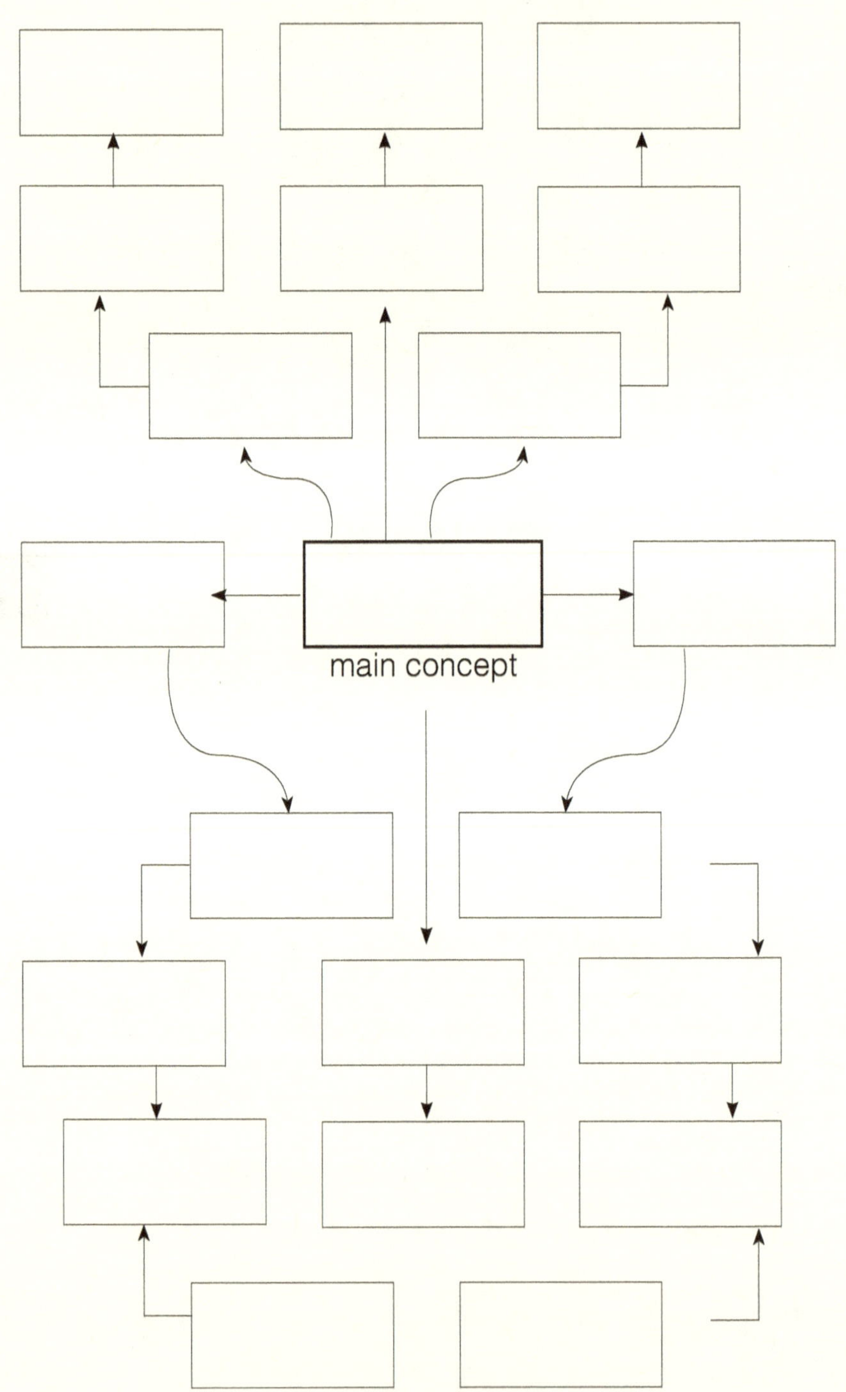

Organize Your Thoughts
(from the concept web)

Thumbnails

Brain Exhausted?

Let your intuition guide you.
Write down the first word that comes to mind for each word on the list.

Animal _______________________________

Clothing _______________________________

Color _______________________________

State _______________________________

Salary _______________________________

Car _______________________________

Travel _______________________________

Career _______________________________

Book _______________________________

Tool _______________________________

Thumbnails

This is a page of possibilities.

Colors
(create the mood)

Palette #1

Palette #2

Texture/Pattern

Spot Colors

Headline

Subtitle/ Supporting

Body Copy

Repeat After me...
Typography Is Important! Typography Is Important! Typography Is Important!

Graphics & Images
(make a list or sketch ideas)

5

Final Design Choices

Color Palette #1

Headline typeface/font & alignment:

Subtitle typeface/font & alignment:

Body copy typeface/font & alignment:

Graphics

1)   5)

2)   6)

3)   7)

4)   8)

Photographs/Illustrations

1)   5)

2)   6)

3)   7)

4)   8)

Final Sketch

Connect the Dots
and color in the shapes

Project
6

You are the limit to your creativity.

Font: Baskerville Old Face
True Type

Project

Client

Contact Name

Number

Due Date   Budget

What are you producing?

PRINT

Logo   Brochure   Business Card   Infographic   Flyer   PSA

Multi-page Booklet   Postcard   Print Ad   Package Design

Outdoor Advertising   Poster   Vehicle Wrap

Other____

WEB

Social Media Ad   On-line Book   Website   Animated Gif

Web Banner   Video   Powerpoint   Image Correction/s

Other ____

Programs that will be used to build the project.

Illustrator   Photoshop   InDesign   Quark Express

PowerPoint   Premiere   Final Cut Pro   Corel

Other____________________   Program Version ____________

Platform   Mac   PC

What is the purpose of this project? (the objective)

What is the message? (what do you want to say)

6

Where will this product be used?

How will this product or service be used?

When will this product or service be used?

What is the tone of the piece? (use adjectives)

Who is your competition?

Target Audience
Demographics - Gathering Data
Who you want to buy your product or service?

Age

Gender

Ethnicity

Religious Beliefs

Occupation

Income

Interests & Hobbies

Values

Location

Schedule

(keep on task)

Client Brief ___________________________________

Press Date ____________________________________

Concept Web _________________________________

Thumbnails __________________________________

Sketches ____________________________________

Project Presentation ___________________________

First Revisions _______________________________

2nd Revisions ________________________________

Final Revisions ______________________________

File Submission ______________________________

Delivery Date_________________________________

Month ____

Sun	Mon	Tues	Wed	Thur	Fri	Sat

Deadlines are given for a reason. Take them seriously.

Time Clock

Date	Time	Hours worked
/ /		
/ /		
/ /		
/ /		
/ /		
/ /		
/ /		
/ /		
/ /		
/ /		
/ /		

Total amount of hours worked _______________

Are the amount of hours spent on a project = to its success? You tell me.

Project Dimensions and Specs.

in   pica   px   mm   pt

Number of Pages ____

Size H _______________ x W _______________ x D ___________

Size H _______________ x W _______________ x D ___________

Columns _________________   Margins __________________

Bleed __________________   Gutter __________________

Color Mode   CMYK   RGB   Spot Colors

Other_________________________________

File Formats

Print   ai   psd   indd   eps   tiff   pdf

svg   jpeg   other

Web   psd   eps   tiff   gif   png   jpeg

other

DPI ____

Other Specifications/Finishing

spreads   die cut   die   mock up   binding

fold   score   gloss   perforation   matte

template   printer's marks

other ______________________________________

Inspiration

(paste images from magazines, mail or any printed material)

6

Attention Grabbing Components Needed
(fill in content after you brainstorm)

Headline:

Subtitle:

Body Copy:

Slogan/Tagline:

Company Name:

Product Name:

Other:

Brainstorm - Concept Web

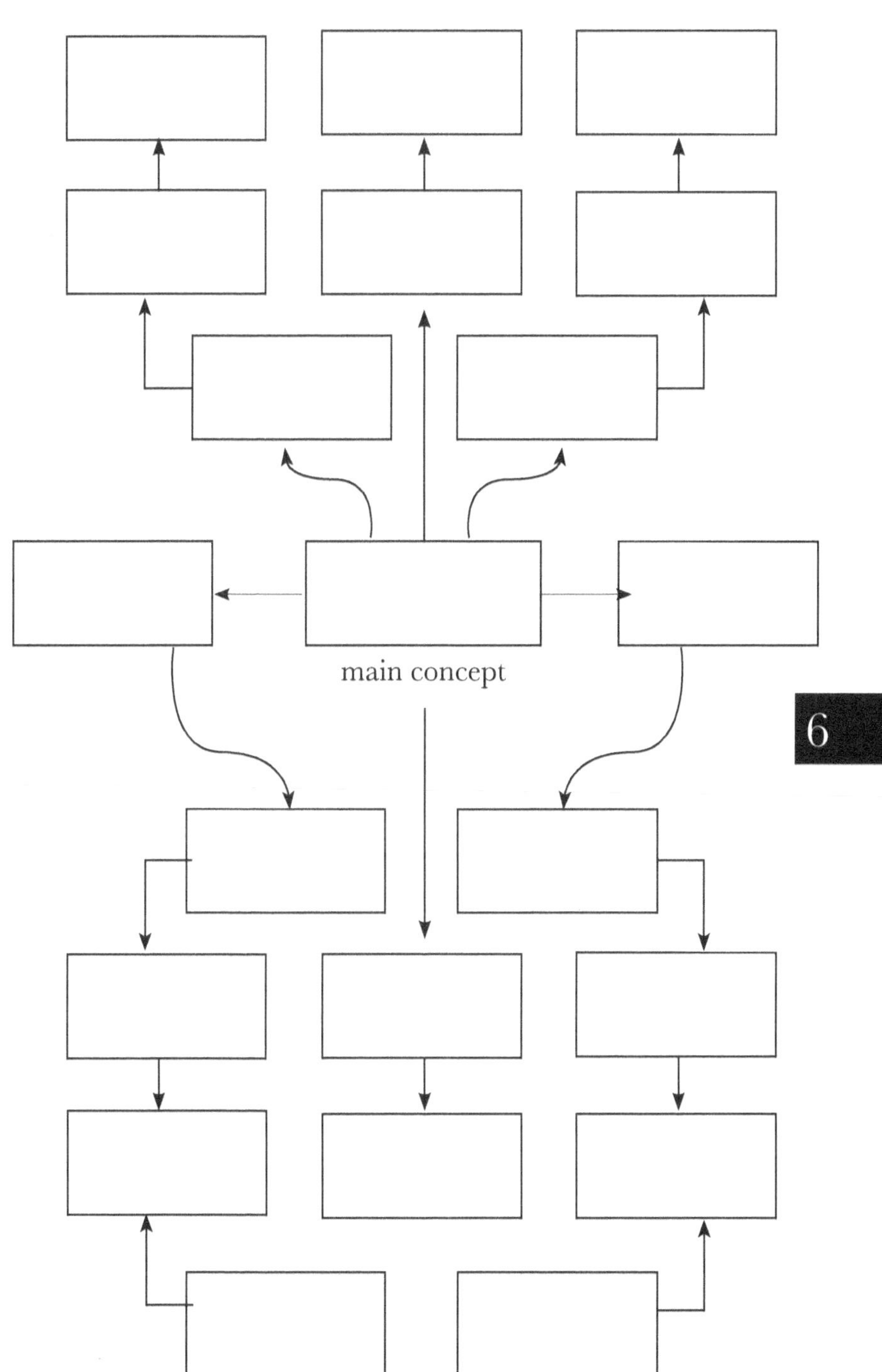

Organize
(final thoughts from concept web)

Organize
(final thoughts from concept web)

Thumbnails

Go for it. A few more thumbnails never hurt anyone.

Music: the catalyst

Put your headphones on and play your favorite song. Draw what is in front of you. Feel the beat. Allow your pencil to keep up with the rhythm.

Thumbnails

Colors
(create the mood)

Palette #1

Palette #2   *Choose colors that you find odd.*

Texture/Pattern

Spot Colors

Headline

Subtitle/ Supporting

6

Body Copy

Graphics & Images

The Final Sketch

6

Final Design Choices

Color Palette

Headline Typeface/Font and Alignment:

Subtitle Typeface/Font and Alignment:

Body Copy Typeface/Font and Alignment:

Graphics

1)   5)

2)   6)

3)   7)

4)   8)

Images/Illustrations

1)   5)

2)   6)

3)   7)

4)   8)

Project
7

You are here for a reason.

Font: Eurostile
Open Type

Project: Due Date

Client:

                                                      Budget

Client contact:

What are you producing?

Print

Logo   Brochure   Business Card   PSA

Infographic   Flyer   Multi-page Booklet   Postcard

Print Ad   Package Design   Outdoor Advertising

Poster   Vehicle Wrap   Letterhead/Envelope

Other_______________________________________

Web

Social Media Ad   On-line Book   Website   Animated Gif

Web banner   Video   Powerpoint   Image Corrections

Other ____

Programs that will be used to build the project.

Illustrator   Photoshop   InDesign   Quark Express

PowerPoint   Premiere   Final Cut Pro   Corel

Other___________________Program Version ____________

Platform   Mac   PC

What is the purpose? (the objective)

What is the message? (what do you want to say)

7

Where will this product be used?

How will this product be used?

When will this product be used?

What is the tone of the piece? (use adjectives)

Who is your competition?

Who Is Your Target Audience?

Demographics - Gathering Data

Who do you want to buy your product or service?

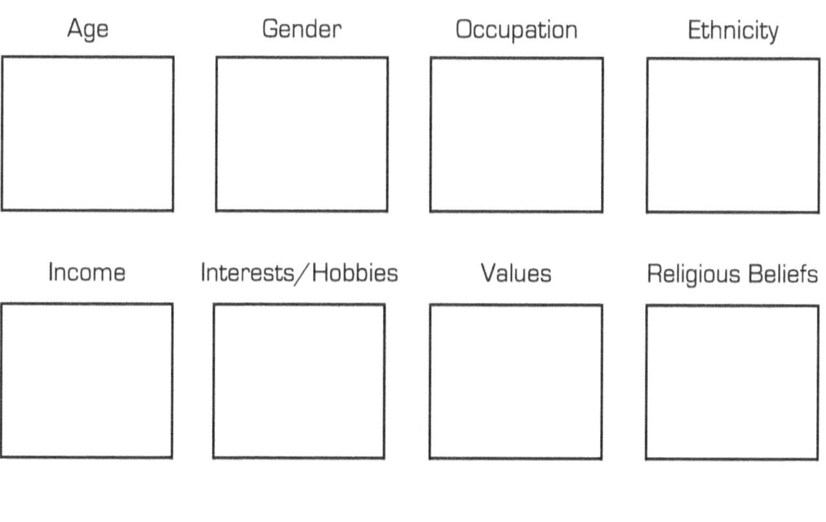

Location - Suburbia, Rural, Metropolitan

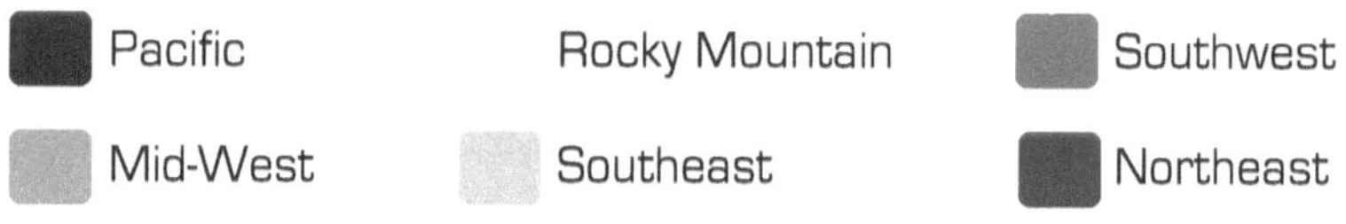

Icecream can be sold anywhere.

Schedule

❶ Client Brief _______________________________

❷ Press Date _______________________________

❸ Concept Web _______________________________

❹ Thumbnails _______________________________

❺ Sketches _______________________________

❻ Project Presentation_______________________________

❼ 1st Revisions _______________________________

❽ 2nd Revisions _______________________________

❾ File Submission _______________________________

❿ Delivery Date _______________________________

Log Your Hours

Date	Time	Hours worked
/ /	__________________	__________
/ /	__________________	__________
/ /	__________________	__________
/ /	__________________	__________
/ /	__________________	__________
/ /	__________________	__________
/ /	__________________	__________
/ /	__________________	__________
/ /	__________________	__________
/ /	__________________	__________
/ /	__________________	__________
/ /	__________________	__________
/ /	__________________	__________

Total hours worked

Project Dimensions and Specs.

in   pica   px   mm   pt

Number of Pages ____

Size   H _________________ x W _________________ x D_____________

Size   H _________________ x W _________________ x D_____________

Columns _________________   Margins _____________________

Bleed _____________________ Gutter _____________________

Color Mode   CMYK   RGB   Spot Colors   Other_____________

File Formats

Print   ai   psd   indd   eps   tiff

pdf   svg   jpeg   other_____________________

Web   psd   eps   tiff   gif   png   jpeg

other____

DPI ____

Other specifications/ Finishing

spreads   die cut   die   mock up   fold

binding   score   gloss   perforation   matte

template   printer's marks

other ________________________________

Inspiration

(paste images from magazines, mail or any printed material)

7

Texture has the ability to evoke emotions and transport the viewer to a specific place.

Attention Grabbing Components Needed
(fill in content after you brainstorm)

Headline:

Subtitle:

Body Copy:

Slogan/Tagline:

Company Name:

Product Name:

Other:

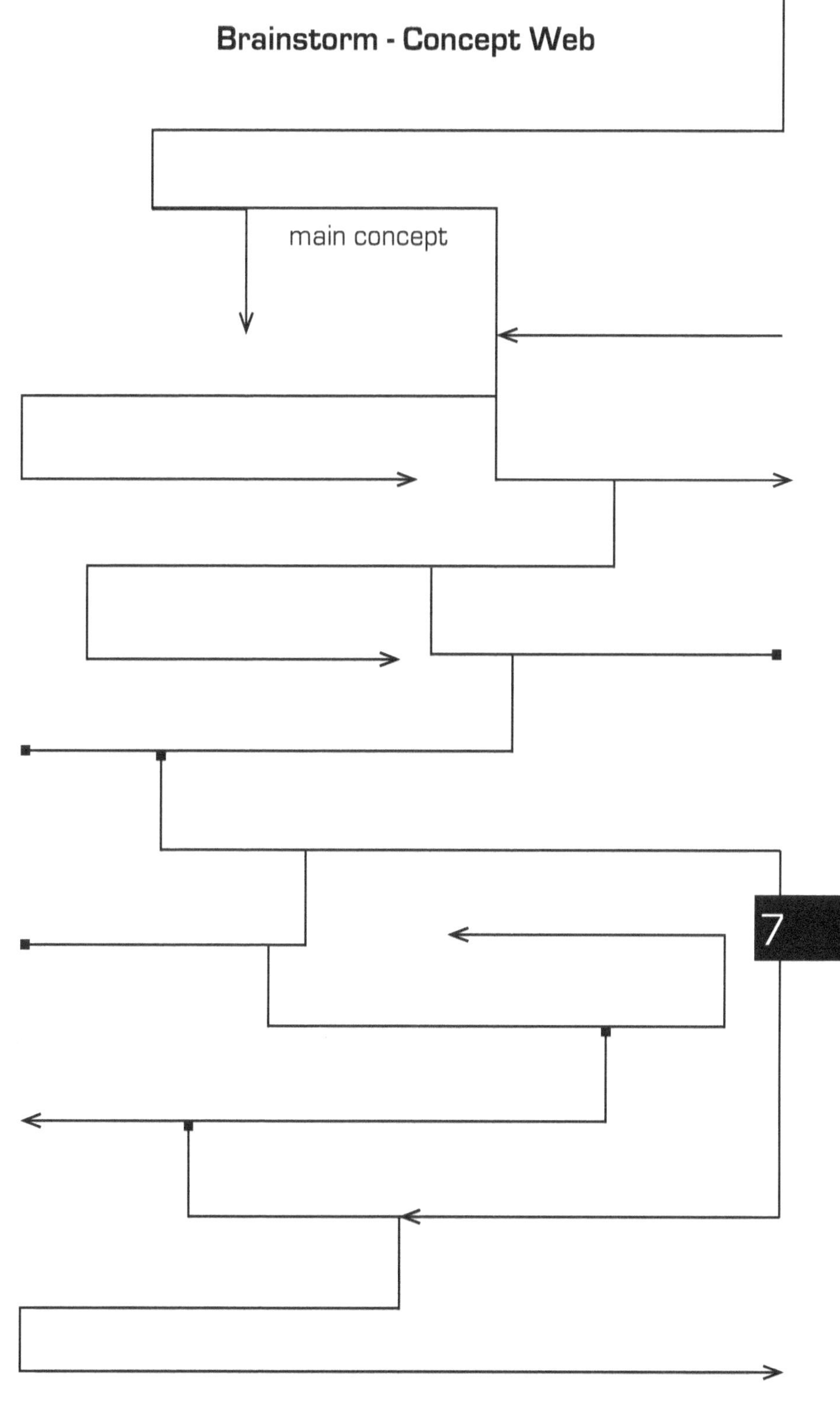
Brainstorm - Concept Web
main concept
main concept
7

Putting It Together
(organize your thoughts from the concept web)

Thumbnails

Brain Exhausted?

Close your eyes for 5 minutes and do nothing.

Thumbnails
(keep going, the more the better)

Any one can think up a good idea on the first try. However a good designer has the ability to go beyond that initial concept and create something unique that will make an impact. There's a difference. Do the work, the rewards are great.

Colors
(create the mood)

Palette #1

Palette #2

Texture/Pattern

Spot Colors

Palette #1 _______ _______ _______ _______

Typefaces/Fonts

Headline

Subtitle/ Supporting

Body Copy

If you have to place a stroke on a font so it can be seen then it's not working. Some people may disagree. Do you? Graphic designers are problem solvers, find a better way.

Graphics & Images

Final Sketch

A final sketch has more detail than a thumbnail. It shows the style of font, color, and placement of elements.

Final Design Choices

Color Palette #1

PMS

____

Headline Typeface

Subtitle Typeface

Body Copy Typeface

Graphics

1)   5)

2)   6)

3)   7)

4)   8)

Photographs/Illustrations

1)   5)

2)   6)

3)   7)

4)   8)

Project

8

Look around, *Graphic Design is a real career.* It may not solve a world crisis, but we do need people to design protest posters, propaganda phamplets, newspapers, social media ads and animated gifs to get the word out.

Font: Bodoni 72 Old Style
True Type

Project:

Due Date

Client:

Client contact:

What are you producing?

Print

Logo   Brochure   Business Card   PSA   Flyer

Infographic   Multi-page Booklet   Postcard   Print Ad

Package Design   Outdoor Advertising   Poster

Vehicle Wrap   Character Design

Other_______________________________________

Web

Social Media Ad   On-line Book   Website   Animated Gif

Web Banner   Video   Powerpoint   Image Correction/s

Other_______________________________________

Programs that will be used to build the project.

Illustrator   Photoshop   InDesign   Quark Express

PowerPoint   Premiere   Final Cut Pro   Corel

Other____________________ Program Version _________

Platform: Mac PC

What is the purpose? (the objective)

What is the message? (what do you want to say)

Where will this product be used?

8

How will this product be used?

When will this product be used?

What is the tone of the piece? (use adjectives)

Who is your competition?

Who Is Your Target Audience?

Demographics - Gathering Data

Who do you want to buy your product or service?

Age	Gender	Occupation	Ethnicity

Income	Interests/Hobbies	Values	Religious Beliefs

Location - Suburbia, Farm, City, Homeless

- Pacific
- Rocky Mountain
- Southwest
- Mid-West
- Southeast
- Northeast

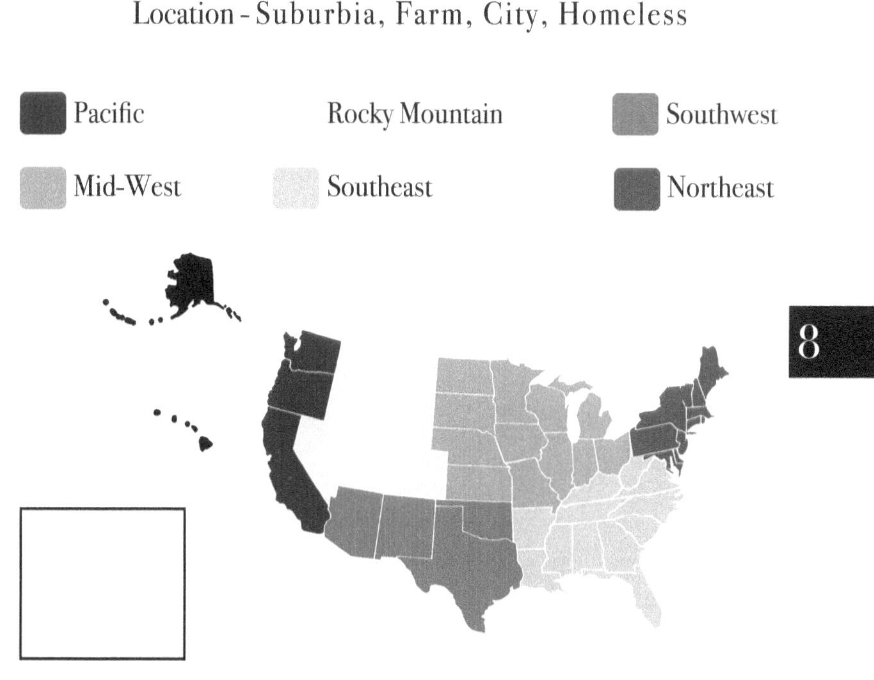

Schedule
(due dates)

Client Brief ____________________________

Press Date __________________________

Concept Web ________________________

Thumbnails __________________________

Sketches ____________________________

Project Presentation _________________

First Round Revisions ________________

2nd Round Revisions _________________

Final Revisions _____________________

File Submissions ___________________

Delivery Date_________________________

Time Sheet

Date	Time	Total hours worked
/ /	______________________	______________
/ /	______________________	______________
/ /	______________________	______________
/ /	______________________	______________
/ /	______________________	______________
/ /	______________________	______________
/ /	______________________	______________
/ /	______________________	______________
/ /	______________________	______________
/ /	______________________	______________
/ /	______________________	______________
/ /	______________________	______________
/ /	______________________	______________

Total amount of hours worked

Project Dimensions and Specs.

in   pica   px   mm   pt

Number of Pages ____

Size H ________________ x W ________________ x D____________

Size H ________________ x W ________________ x D____________

Columns ____________________   Margins ____________________

Bleed ______________________ Gutter ____________________

Color Mode   CMYK   RGB   Spot Colors   Other__________________

File Formats

Print   ai   psd   indd   eps   tiff

pdf   svg   jpeg   other______________________________

Web   psd   eps   tiff   gif   png   jpeg

other____

DPI ____

Other Specifications/ Finishing

spreads   template   die cut   die   mock up

binding   fold   score   perforation   gloss   matte

printer's marks   other____________________________

Inspiration

Know your surroundings. What types of signs did you notice on your way here today.

Attention Grabbing Components Needed
(fill in content after you brainstorm)

Headline:

Subtitle:

Body Copy:

Slogan/Tagline:

Company Name:

Product Name:

Other:

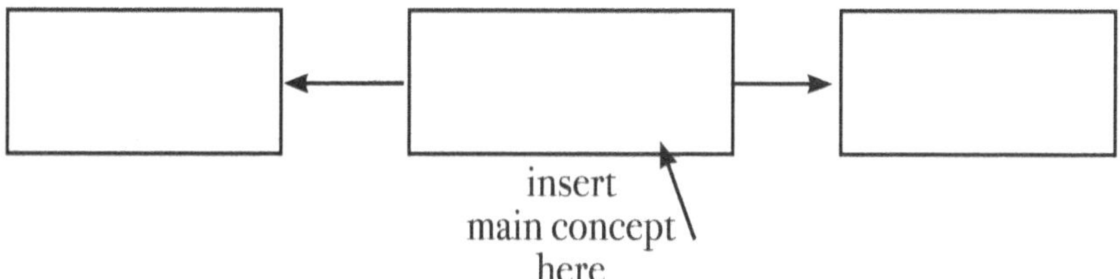
insert
main concept
here

Organize Your Thoughts
(from concept web)

Thumbnails

X Marks the Spot

Where would you hide a treasure? Think of a place and create a map for someone else to follow.

More Thumbnails
(yes, more thumbnails)

Notes

Colors
(create the mood)

Palette #1

Palette #2

Texture/Pattern

Spot Colors

Typefaces/Fonts

Headline Fonts

Subtitle/ Supporting Fonts

Body Copy Fonts

Take personal taste out of choosing fonts. You will be much more successful.

Graphics & Images
(make a list or sketch ideas)

Color Sketch

Final Design Choices

Color Palette #1

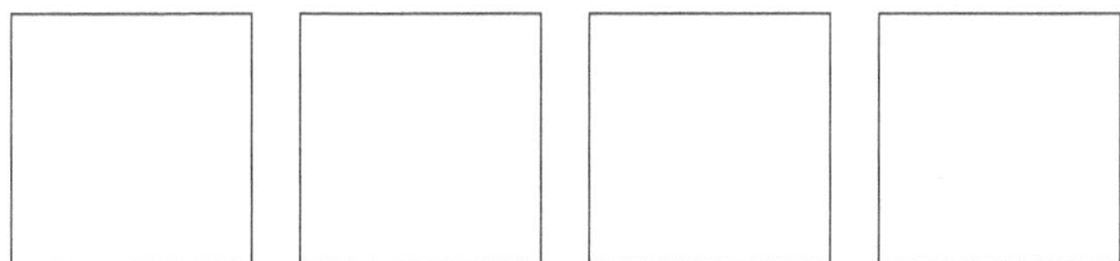

Headline Font: ______________________________ FR   FL   C   J

Subtitle Font: ______________________________ FR   FL   C   J

Body Copy Font: ______________________________ FR   FL   C   J

Graphics

1)   5)

2)   6)

3)   7)

4)   8)

Images/Illustrations

1)   5)

2)   6)

3)   7)

4)   8)

Mindlessly Scribble

Project
9

How will you
change design?

How will design
change you?

Font: Consolas
Open Type

Project: Due Date

Client:

                                            Budget

Client contact:

What are you producing?

Print

Logo   Brochure   Business Card   PSA   Infographic

Flyer   Multi-page Booklet   Postcard   Print Ad

Package Design   Outdoor Advertising   Poster

Vehicle Wrap   Character Design

Other____

Web

Social Media Ad   On-line Book   Website   Animated Gif

Web Banner   Video   Powerpoint   Image Corrections

Other ____

Programs that will be used to build the project.

Illustrator   Photoshop   InDesign   Quark Express

PowerPoint   Premiere   Final Cut Pro   Corel

Other__________________ Program Version __________

➪**Platform   Mac   PC**

What is the purpose? (the objective)

What is the message? (what do you want to say)

Where will this product be used?

How will this product be used?

When will this product be used?

What is the tone of the piece? (use adjectives)

Who is your competition?

Who Is Your Target Audience?

Demographics - Gathering Data

Who do you want to buy your product or service?

Age

Gender

Occupation

Ethnicity

Income

Interests/Hobbies

Values

Religious Beliefs

Location - Suburbia, Rural, Metropolitan

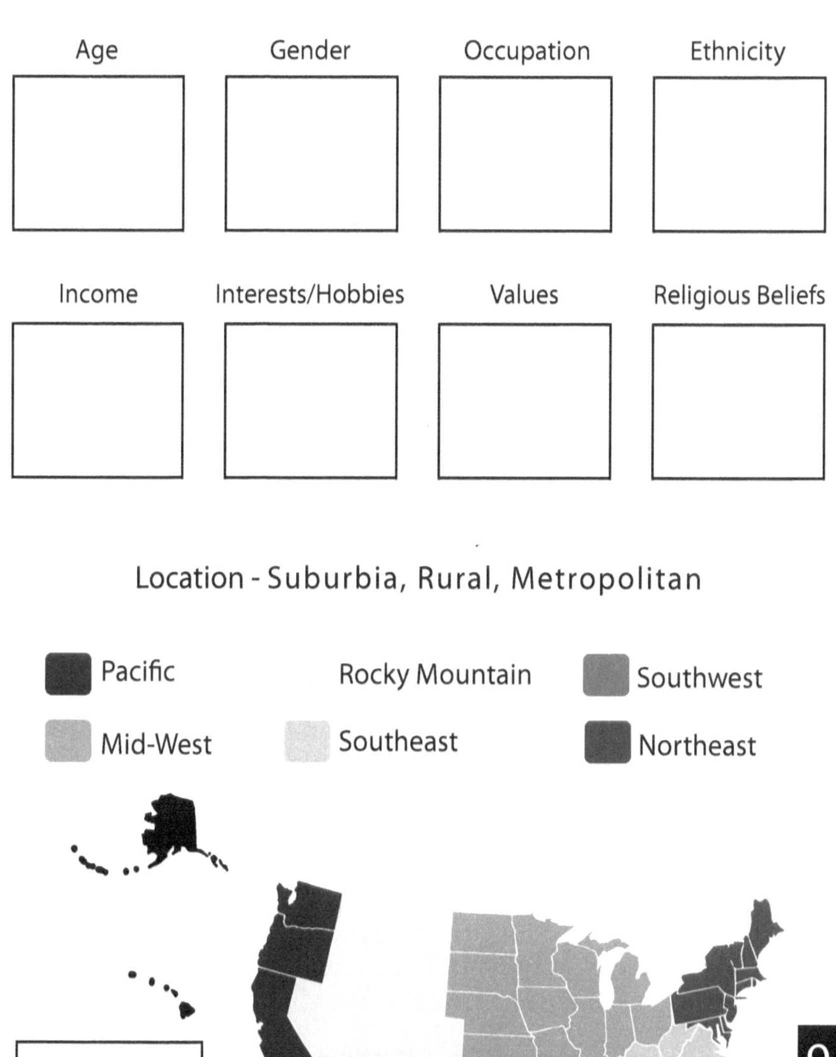

Schedule
(due dates)

Client Brief _______________________________

Press Date _______________________________

Concept Web _______________________________

Thumbnails _______________________________

Sketches _______________________________

Project Presentation _______________________________

First Round Revisions _______________________________

2nd Round Revisions _______________________________

Final Revisions _______________________________

Final File Submissions _______________________________

Delivery Date_______________________________

Time Sheet

Date	Time	Hours worked
/ /	_________________	_________
/ /	_________________	_________
/ /	_________________	_________
/ /	_________________	_________
/ /	_________________	_________
/ /	_________________	_________
/ /	_________________	_________
/ /	_________________	_________
/ /	_________________	_________
/ /	_________________	_________
/ /	_________________	_________
/ /	_________________	_________

Total hours worked _________

Project Dimensions and Specs.

in   pica   px   mm   pt

Number of Pages ____

Size H _______________ x W _______________ x D_______________

Size H _______________ x W _______________ x D_______________

Columns _________________   Margins_____________________

Bleed _________________   Gutter _____________________

Color Mode   CMYK   RGB   Spot Colors   Other __________

File Formats

Print   ai   psd   indd   eps   tiff

          pdf   svg   jpeg   other _______________

Web   psd   eps   tiff   gif   png   jpeg

          other_______________________

DPI ____

Other Specifications/ Finishing

          spreads   template   die cut   die   mock up

          binding   fold   score   perforation   gloss

          matte   printer's marks: crop/registration/bleed

          other_______________________

Inspiration

If you use Photoshop to alter the appearance of a product, is it considered false advertising?

Attention Grabbing Components Needed
(fill in content after you brainstorm)

Headline:

Subtitle:

Body Copy:

Slogan/Tagline:

Company Name:

Product Name:

Other:

Brainstorm - Concept Web

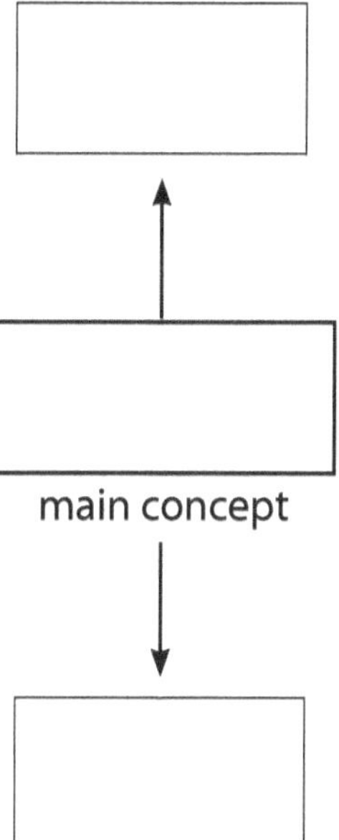

9

Take a Break and Eat

Eating healthy plays a crucial role in proper brain function that is necessary for creative thinking and problem solving.

Match the artist to the food
What food is each artist known
for in their art?

Paul Cezanne	Lobster
Andy Warhol	Apples
Norman Rockwell	Milk
Vincent Van Gogh	Potatoes
Johannes Vermeer	Tomato Soup
René Magritte	Turkey
Willem Kalf	Fruit

Organize Your Ideas
(final thoughts from the concept web)

Thumbnails

One does not have to fill up the page with useless stuff. Keep it simple.....

9

Colors
(create the mood)

Palette #1

Palette #2

Texture/Pattern

Spot Colors

Palette #1

Typefaces/Fonts

Headline

Subtitle/ Supporting

Body Copy

Sketch

What type of image is appropriate to communicate the message?

9

Final Design Choices

Color Palette #1

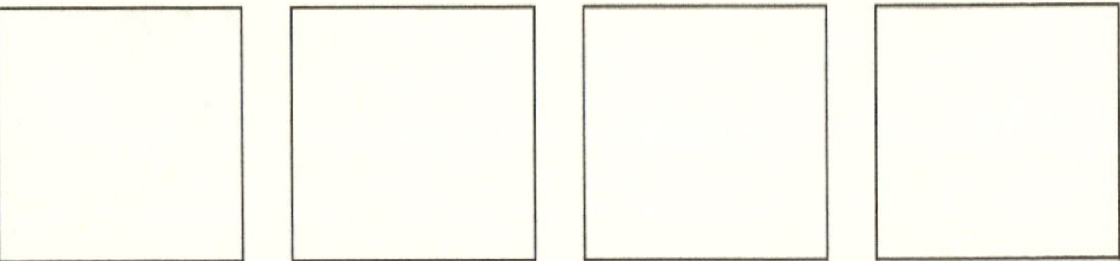

Headline Font: _______________________________ FR   FL   C   J

Subtitle Font: _______________________________ FR   FL   C   J

Body Copy Font: _____________________________ FR   FL   C   J

Graphics

1)   5)

2)   6)

3)   7)

4)   8)

Photographs/Illustrations

1)   5)

2)   6)

3)   7)

4)   8)

Project
X

Digital Design
Animated Gif, Video

Font: Futura Medium
Open Type

Project: Due Date

Client:

                                            Budget

Client contact:

What digital media are you producing?

Animated Gif   Video

Other____

Is this Project for a Product or Service? _______________________

Media: Web Banner   PSA   Infomercial

Other____

Topic:____

Programs that will be used to build the project.

Illustrator   Photoshop   InDesign   Quark Express

PowerPoint   Premiere   Final Cut Pro   Corel

Other_________________   Program Version _________

Platform: Mac   PC

What is the purpose? (the objective)

What is the message? (what do you want to say)

Where will this be seen?

X

When will this be seen? (specific time slot on web, a webpage, pop up ad, etc)

How do you want this to be perceived?

What is the tone of the piece? (use adjectives)

Who is your competition?

Who Is Your Target Audience?

Demographics - Gathering Data

Who do you want to buy your product or service?

Age	Gender	Occupation	Ethnicity

Income	Interests & Hobbies	Values	Religious Beliefs

Location: Suburbia   Rural   Metropolitan

USA

■ Pacific   Rocky Mountain   ■ Southwest

■ Mid-West   Southeast   ■ Northeast

Europe   Asia   Middle East   Austrialia   South Pole

South America   Central America   Africa   Canada

How does one solve the problem of language barriers? **X**

Schedule

Client Brief ________________________________

Air Date ________________________________

Concept Web ________________________________

Storyboard ________________________________

Audio ________________________________

Project Presentation__________________________

First Revisions____________________________

2nd Revisions____________________________

Final File Submission_________________________

Due Date ________________________________

Time Sheet

Date	Time	Hours worked
/ /		
/ /		
/ /		
/ /		
/ /		
/ /		
/ /		
/ /		
/ /		
/ /		
/ /		
/ /		

Total Hours ___________

Project Dimensions and Specs.

Pixels   RGB

Length of video ___________________________

File Size: Animated Gif

___Leaderboard 720 x 90

___Full Banner 468 x 60

___Square Pop Up 250 x250

___Wide Skyscraper160 x 600

___Other__________________________

Frames per second ___________

File Size: Video

___1080p 1920 x 1080

___ 720p 1280 x 720

___Other__________________________

Frames per second___________

File Formats:

___AVI   ___Flash   ___WMV   ___QuickTime

___MP4   Other_________________________________

Inspiration

Attention Grabbing Components Needed
(fill in content after you brainstorm)

Title:

Headline:

Subtitle:

Body Copy:

Slogan/Tagline:

Logo:

Other:

Brainstorm - Concept Web

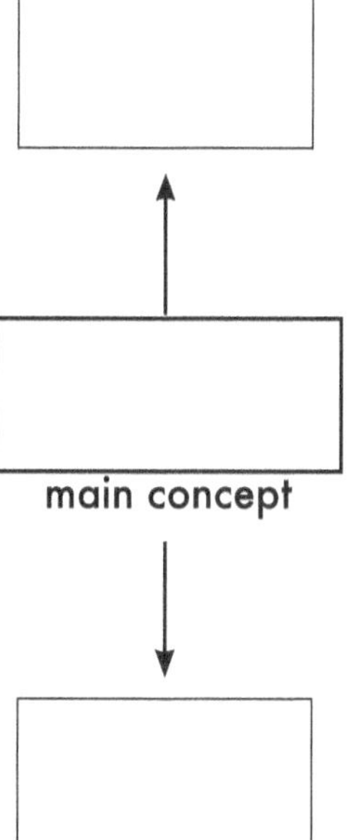

Movie Time

Movies that will increase your knowledge
and stimulate your creativity.

Match the artist to the movie.

Paul Giamatti	The Agony and the Escasty
Frida Kahlo	American Splendor
Michel Angelo	Exit Through the Gift Shop
Vincent Van Gogh	Downtown 81
Johannes Vermeer	Frida
Bansky	Girl with a Pearl Earring
Jean Michael Basquiat	Lust for Life

Pick one of the above and watch this weekend.

Putting It Together
(final thoughts from concept web)

Colors & Setting
(create the mood)

Palette #1

Mood (happy, festive, somber) _______________________________

Colors

Background (solid color, gradient, pattern_______________________________

Location (school, playground, beach) _______________________________

Palette #2

Mood (happy, festive, somber) _______________________________

Colors

Background (solid color, gradient, pattern_______________________________

Location (school, playground, beach) _______________________________

Palette #3

Mood (happy, festive, somber) _______________________________

Colors

Background (solid color, gradient, pattern_______________________________

Location (school, playground, beach) _______________________________

Character One Development

Age	Gender	Ethnicity

Character Description

    hair color-

    hair style-

    eye color-

    body shape-

What is character wearing?

How does character feel?

How does character act?

Character Two Development

Age	Gender	Ethnicity

Character Description

hair color-

hair style-

eye color-

body shape-

What is character wearing?

How does character feel?

How does character act?

Supporting Character Development

<table>
<tr><td>Age</td><td>Gender</td><td>Ethnicity</td></tr>
<tr><td>

</td><td>

</td><td>

</td></tr>
</table>

Character Descriptions

    hair color-

    hair style-

    eye color-

    body shape-

What are characters wearing?

How are characters feeling?

How are characters acting?

Storyboard 1

Time

Action

Time

Action

Storyboard 2

Time

Action

Time

Action

Storyboard 3

Time

Action

Time

Action

Storyboard 4

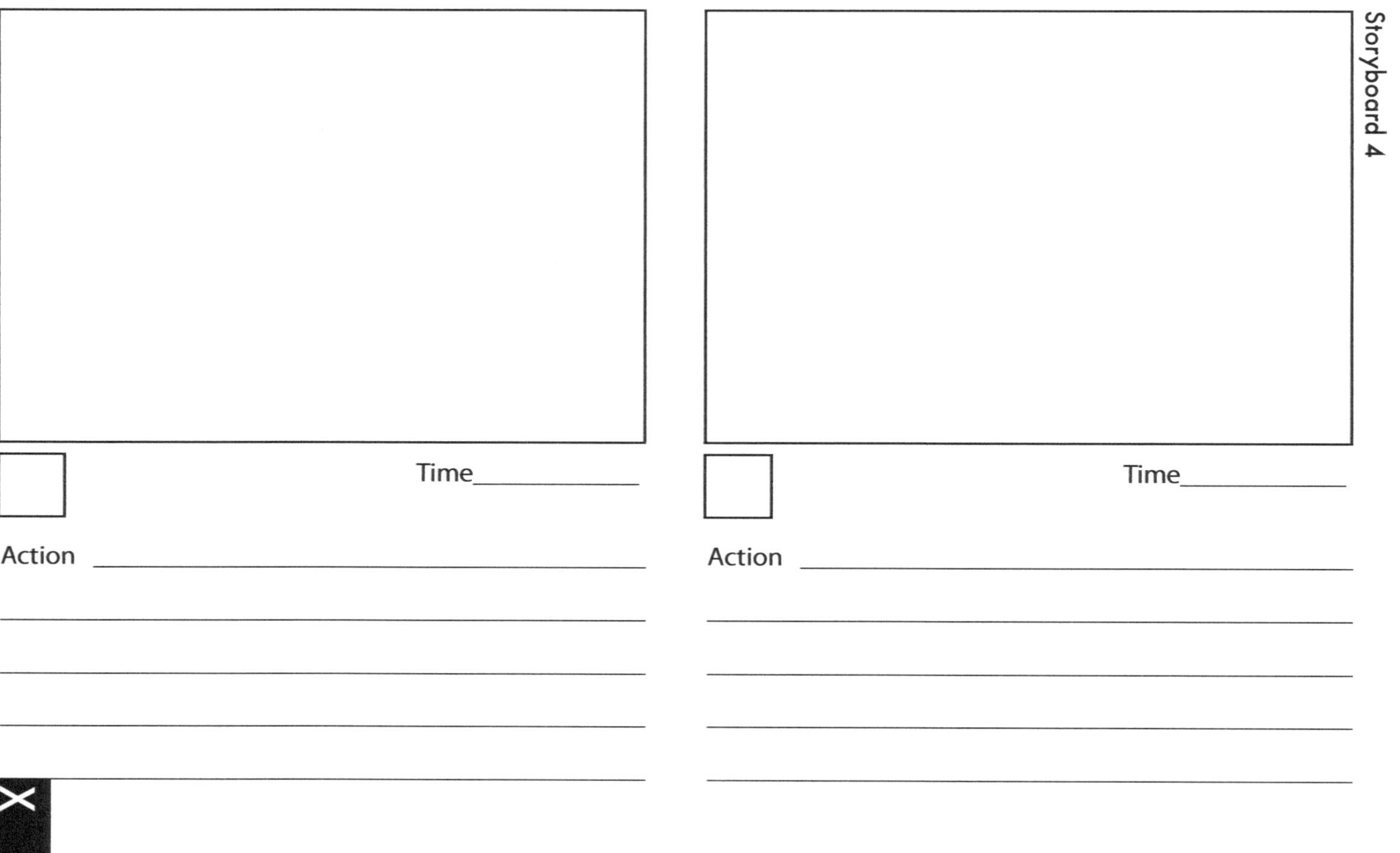

Storyboard 5

Time

Action

Time

Action

Audio 1

Frame ☐

Dialogue____

____

____

Music/Sound ____

Frame ☐

Dialogue____

____

____

Music/Sound ____

Frame ☐

Dialogue____

____

____

Music/Sound ____

Frame ☐

Dialogue____

____

____

Music/Sound ____

X

Audio 2

Frame ☐

Dialogue____

____

____

Music/Sound ____

Frame ☐

Dialogue____

____

____

Music/Sound ____

Frame ☐

Dialogue____

____

____

Music/Sound ____

Frame ☐

Dialogue____

____

____

Music/Sound ____

Audio 3

Frame [ ]

Dialogue_______________________________

____

____

Music/Sound ____________________________

Frame [ ]

Dialogue_______________________________

____

____

Music/Sound ____________________________

Frame [ ]

Dialogue_______________________________

____

____

Music/Sound ____________________________

Frame [ ]

Dialogue_______________________________

____

____

Music/Sound ____________________________

X

Final Design Choices

Color Palette #1

Character/s:

#1 ____

#2 ____

#3 ____

Setting: ____

Mood: ____

Title Font: ______________________________ FR FL C J

Text effect ______________________________________

Subtitle Font: ___________________________ FR FL C J

Text effect ______________________________________

Body Copy Font: _________________________ FR FL C J

Text effect ______________________________________

Credits:

Brain Exhausted?
Mindlessly Scribble

X

Graphic Design Basics

Graphic Design Terminology

Graphic Design Elements
The physical components of a composition

Line
Shape
Color
Typography
Space
Texture
Form
Value

Principles of Design
How the physical components of a composition are applied

Hierarchy
Emphasis
Balance
Alignment
Contrast
Proportion/Scale
Repetition
Rhythm
Flow

Color Theory
The Science of color relationships

Additive - RGB
Subtractive - CMYK
Primary
Secondary
Tertiary
Value
Monochromatic
Complementary
Triadic
Analogous
Split complementary
Warm
Cool
Tint
Shade

Laws of Gestalt
"Unified Whole"
The Psychology of visual perception in graphic design

Law of Proximity
Law of Similarity
Law of Continuity
Law of Closure
Law of Figure/Ground

Printers Marks

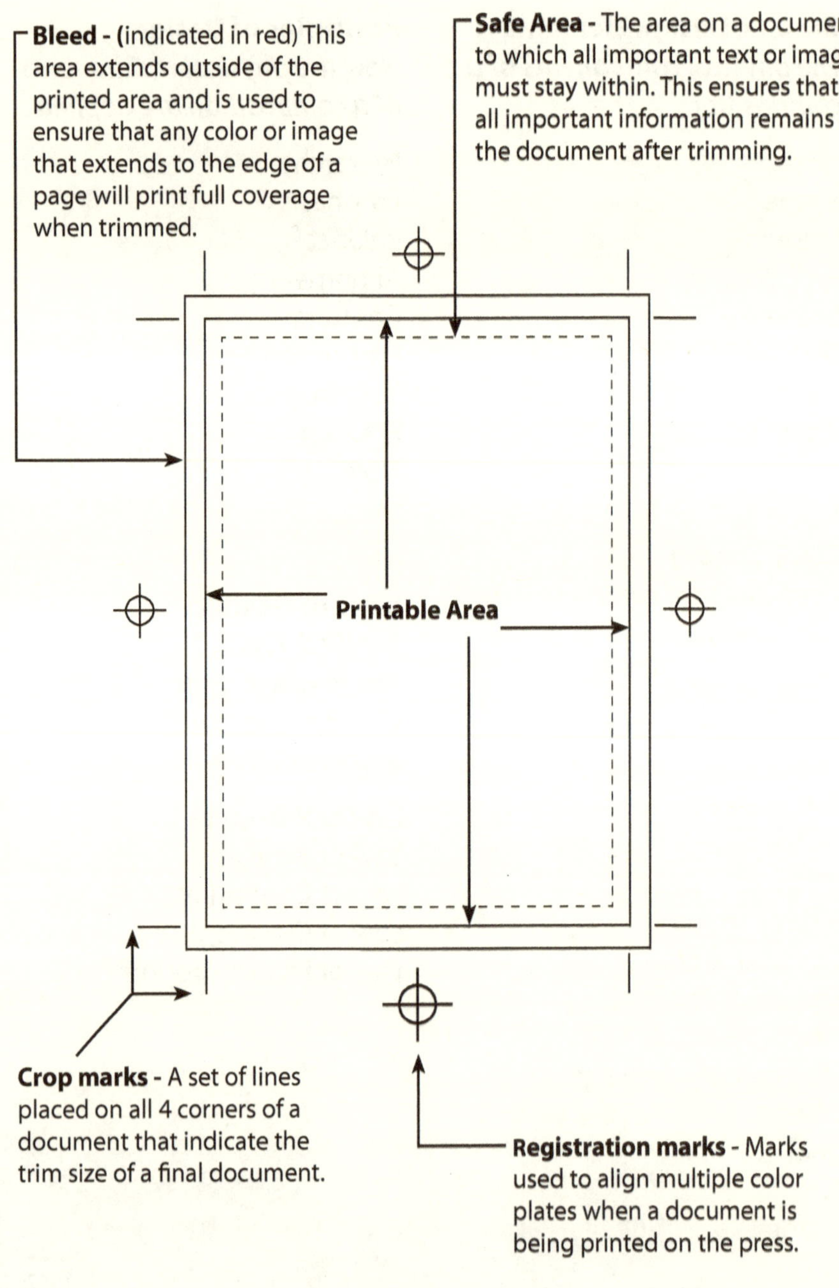

Color

Color is a powerful element in graphic design. It sets the mood, attracts attention, evokes feelings and emotions, and communicates messages. As a designer, by understanding color and how different cultures perceive color, will enable you to achieve effective results.

Subtractive Color (CMYK) ⇨ Ink
　　Printing inks used in four color process printing.
　　C-Cyan
　　M-Magenta
　　Y-Yellow
　　K-Key the (black) plate to which all colors are aligned.

Additive Color (RGB) ⇨ Light
　　Computer Monitor
　　R-Red
　　G-Green
　　B-Blue

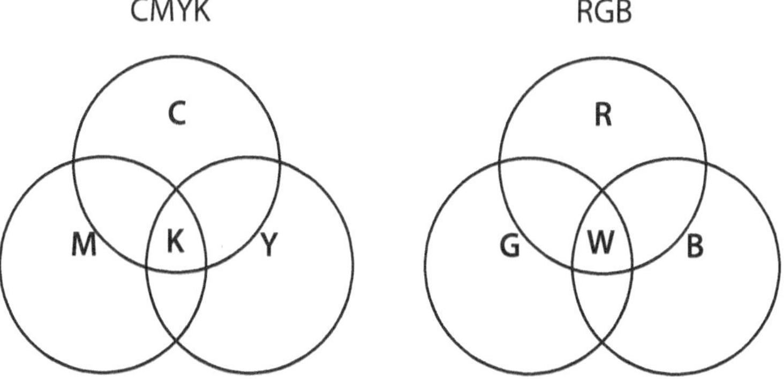

Color Wheel

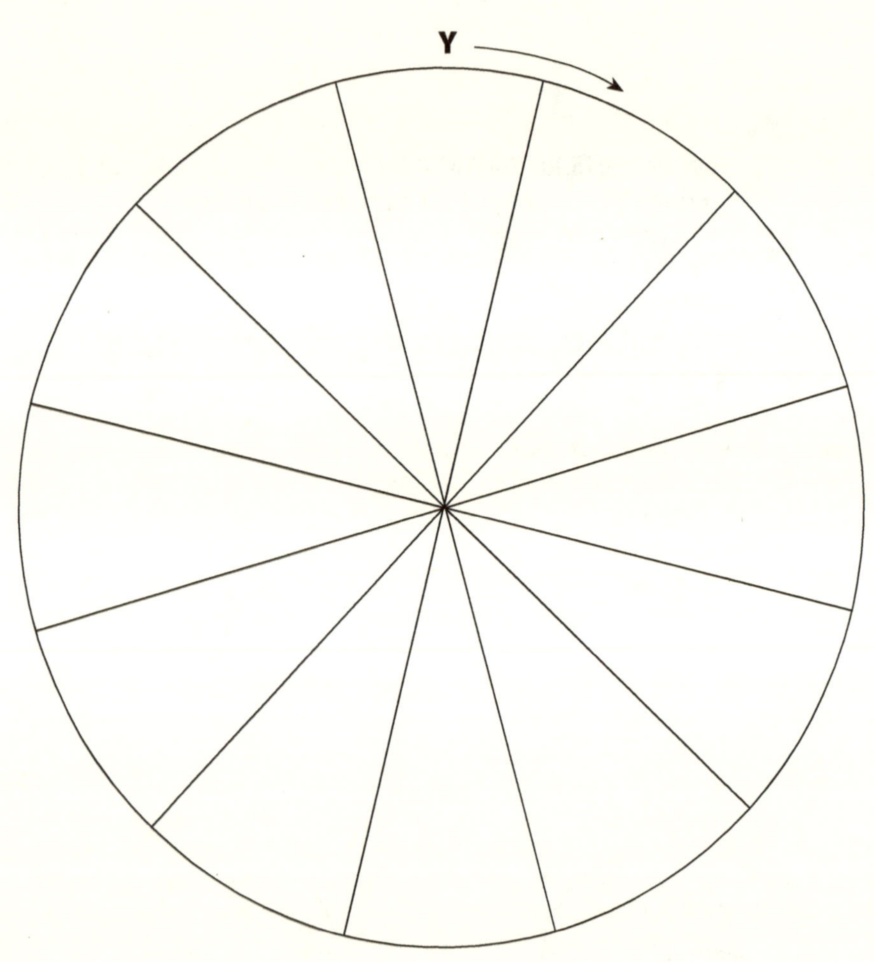

Using colored pencils, fill in and label each section of the color wheel according to your research. Start with Y=yellow.

Color Theory

Primary

Secondary

Tertiary

Complementary

Analogous

Split Complementary

Color Theory

Triadic

Tetradic

Warm

Cool

Grayscale

Monochromatic

Tints-

Shades-

Typeface Categories

Calligraphic	*Monotype Corsiva* *Apple Chancery* **Blackmoor LET** *Zapfino*
Old Style	Garamond
Transitional	Baskerville
Modern	**Bodoni**
Egyptian	**Playbill**
Script	*Snell Roundhand* *Brush Script MT*
Sanserif	Helvetica Gill Sans Century Gothic **Futura**
Decorative	ROSEWOOD MESQUITE Rothenburg Decorati

TYPE DISSECTION
Type Terminology

Points -   A form of measurement for type, and line thickness (72 pts per inch). (pts)

Picas -   A form of measurement for line length.

Leading - Space between the lines of text measured from baseline to baseline.

Kerning - The process of adjusting the space between two characters.

Tracking - The process of adjusting the spacing between all characters of selected text.

Alignment

Flush Right |Ragged Left

> This text is Minion Pro Regular, 10/12pt and has a Flush Right/Ragged Left alignment.

Flush Left | Ragged Right

> This text is Minion Pro Regular, 10/12pt and has a Flush Left/Ragged Right alignment.

Justified

> This text is Minion Pro Regular, 10/12pt and has a Justified alignment.

Centered

> This text is Minion Pro Regular, 10/12pt and has a Centered alignment.

Minion Pro Font Styles

Bold Cond

Bold Cond Italic

Regular

Italic

Medium

Medium Italic

Semi Bold

Semibold Italic

Bold

Bold Italic

Minion Pro
150 pts

Bodini 72
150 pts

Helvetica
150 pts

Serif vs. Sans Serif

Distinguishable letter parts of the letter **"s"**

TYPE DISSECTION

Edwardian Script

type master

TYPE DISSECTION
Garamond Font Family

34
ABCDEFG
abcdefg
hijklmnopqrstuvwxyz
GHIJKLMNOPQRSTUVWXYZ

012
567

Descender
Baseline
Ascender

Ab xahp
Upper Case
Lower Case
x-height

Garamond

G

Font Styles
Garamond Regular
Garamond Italic
Garamond **Bold**
Garamond ***Bold Italic***

89

Distinguishable parts of the lowercase "e"

TYPE DISSECTION

Body Copy & Leading

Garamond 10 | 12pt quamus moluptatet est voluptatin est et a conseque necabo. Hiliquiam quam quatiae vellori onsequis etur? Cil etur? Ores enis dundaessimi, nonse nis eribusae voluptat qui cullaborum.

Bodoni Old Style 10 | 12pt tem aut ario. Nam faccus autem ipsam dolore sitatat ioritent verruptam eariam, in nempori blaudictur, sequas dellacea abo. Raecus quist, ut omnia quissunt pe nullesedi numqui blatur?

Palantino 10 | 12pt secto tet, alissin ctatur aut ratia aligniatem que es maximporem excernam dendand eliquid molorunt omnis dolorecus et quatur reiurecte cus. Magnam conecum et litibus ciamus earitio blam, num accatias et. omnimusdoluptatenis

Minion Pro 10|12pt sed molo eos recte comnimi lluptassinci doluptaquia sum erorum laut ipsaped ipsaeca temporehento officiatio conem quiam fugitatiis.

Helvetica 10l12pt-Henisint di aut voluptur, od quam, corum es entia plabor accaboria volupti umquist, unt molorestrum quatior eritas a parchilis dem quid quo eatationsed molu.

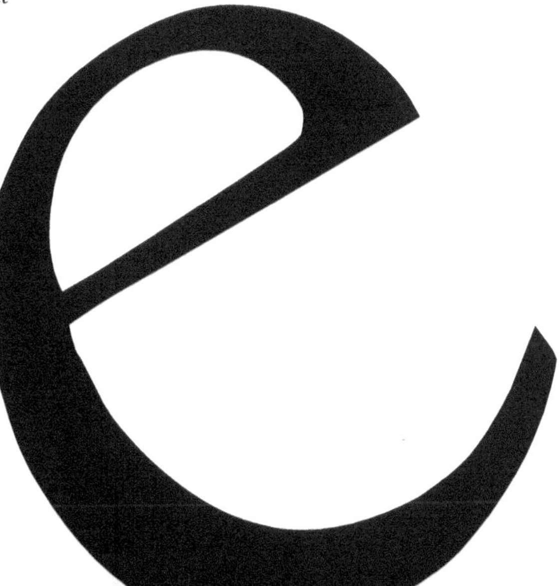

Ruler

Rule Gauge - measured in Points

Hairline

.5
1
2
3
4
6
8
10
12

Baseline

Leading: the space between the
lines of copy measured in points
(pts) from baseline to baseline.

6

7

Rule #1

8

⇨Standard **leading** for body copy is
2 to 3pts. more than the font size.
*The default leading setting on the
computer for a 12pt. font is 14.4pt. (auto)*

9

Rule #2 *fill in your own*

Rule #3

10

11

Rule #4

Leading Gauge

12

13

14

15

Pica Gauge

0 1 2 3 4 5 6 7 8 9 10 11 12 13 14 15 16 17 18 19 20 21 22 23 24 25 26 27 28 29

Answers:

Word Search - pg 55

```
q  y  p  r  i  n  t  n  y  m  o  l  p  r  c  t  g  b  f  t
a  r  t  n  o  u  v  e  a  u  k  m  p  d  w  q  a  n  j  y
s  a  c  i  p  m  o  p  b  s  z  i  r  e  y  t  o  k  h  p
q  c  j  i  e  f  j  n  a  m  l  n  p  r  c  z  g  b  f  o
b  o  d  y  c  o  p  y  u  z  k  i  p  d  w  q  a  n  j  g
y  m  r  v  c  m  o  p  h  w  z  m  a  e  v  e  c  t  o  r
q  p  j  a  e  f  j  c  a  m  o  a  p  n  c  z  g  b  f  a
e  u  a  l  b  m  a  v  u  z  k  l  p  d  b  q  a  n  j  p
y  t  r  v  c  r  o  d  s  w  z  i  r  e  y  m  o  k  h  h
q  e  j  i  e  f  a  n  y  m  o  s  p  r  c  z  u  b  f  y
e  r  a  e  d  n  g  c  i  z  k  m  p  d  w  q  f  h  j  b
y  c  v  p  f  m  o  p  t  w  z  m  r  e  y  i  o  k  t  b
q  r  j  w  e  b  d  e  s  i  g  n  p  r  r  z  g  b  f  t
e  o  a  l  o  m  g  v  i  z  k  o  p  e  w  q  a  n  j  b
y  p  r  v  c  m  o  p  b  w  z  g  s  e  g  e  p  j  h  b
q  m  j  i  n  g  i  s  e  d  c  i  h  p  a  r  g  b  f  q
t  a  r  g  e  t  a  u  d  i  e  n  c  e  w  q  a  n  j  b
y  r  r  v  r  o  m  a  n  t  i  c  i  s  m  t  o  k  h  d
p  k  y  j  i  e  f  j  n  y  m  o  l  p  r  c  z  g  b  a
e  s  a  l  o  m  g  v  i  z  k  f  i  r  e  s  n  a  s  d
y  i  r  a  s  t  e  r  b  w  z  t  n  o  f  t  o  k  h  a
```

Artists & their Movements - pg 73

Paul Cezanne-Post Impressionism • Frida Kahlo-Surrealism • Henri Mattie-Fauvism • Frank Stella-Minimalism • Andy Warhol-Pop Art • Mary Cassett-Impressionism • Alphonse Mucha-Art Deco • Jackson Pollack-Abstract Expressionism • Georges Seurat-Pointillism • Georgia O'Keeffe-American Modernist

Artists & Food - pg 177

Paul Cezanne-Fruit • Andy Warhol-Tomato Soup • Norman Rockwell-Turkey • Vincent Van Gogh-Potatoes • Johannes Vermeer- Milk • René Magrite-Apple • William Kalf-Lobster

*If there is information that you feel needs to be included that may have been overlooked, and would improve the quality of *The Art of the Process* for graphic design students and designers everywhere, send your comments. Have a cover design that you created and would like to see on this book, submit your ideas. > Visit our facebook page @theartoftheprocess